WHAT THINK YE OF
CHRISTMAS?

by ESTER RASBAND

with original watercolor paintings by
JANA WINTERS PARKIN

For Jim
because he believes —

For Jeff
because he gives —

Book design and illustration by Jana Winters Parkin.
Special thanks to Katie Wright for her assistance with the concepts and preliminary sketches. The paintings were created using Daniel Smith, Holbein and Winsor & Newton watercolors on Fabriano Artistico 140# cold press paper. The book is typeset in Adobe Garamond, including Titling Capitals and Italic Alternate characters. Printing by Navigator Cross-Media in Glendale, California. Printed in Korea.

Earlier edition published as *What Think You of Christmas* in 1978 by Bookcraft.

happy holidays

Christ, THEY SAY,
HAS BEEN TAKEN OUT OF
CHRISTMAS.

Small wonder, they say, that some
don't even call it Christmas any more.
His name has been taken from the celebration.

But those who worry themselves over these things
are missing something—

MISSING SOMETHING PERSONAL AND BEAUTIFUL.

Something within their power to have.

CHRISTMAS, LIKE LIFE,
　　IS WHAT YOU MAKE IT.

Because Christmas is a time of *symbols,*
　　Symbols that can give beauty and joy
　　　　to the love that you bring to the Lord.

FOR THE ESSENCE OF CHRISTMAS IS FEELINGS

And in every part of our lives,
     our feelings respond to and with *symbols.*

When words aren't enough, when tender thoughts are deepest,
     A flower, a song,
       the pouring out of heart to heart
         and the need to express is fulfilled.

The Lord understands.

And he gives us symbols by commandment
That we might be touched with remembrance of Him.

*"And behold all things have their likeness, and all
things are created and made to bear record of me, both
things which are temporal and things which are
spiritual; things which are in the heavens above and
things which are in the earth, and things which
are under the earth, both above and beneath:
all things bear record of me."*

And one night, two thousand years ago
Those who refused to despair were rewarded with a *symbol:*

A STAR.

"On the morrow come I into the world."

Every Christmas we remember again that symbol, *that star.*

But if that star we put on our Christmas tree
and cut out of our cookie dough is not
LEADING US TO BETHLEHEM,
it becomes part of a holiday without Christ.

It is our
remembrance of Him
that brings His name
to our celebration.

Bright lights everywhere
are just gaudy
If they do not remind us that

He is the light of the world.

Seeing them must inspire us
to walk in the light,
or his name is missing
in our festival.

Feasting
should remind us of

THE BOUNTY
HE GIVES TO US.

Otherwise
it is just gluttony.

Oᴿᴺᴬᴹᴱᴺᵀˢ
SHOULD REMIND US OF
THE SPLENDOR
that the great Plan of Happiness
brings to our life—

A life that would otherwise be
unadorned—
devoid of both
hope and meaning.

Gifts represent
THE GREATEST GIFT OF ALL
—the gift that came wrapped in
swaddling clothes.

When you give a gift,
are you remembering that
and trying to be like Him?

And it is also blessed to RECEIVE.

Have we not received *God's greatest gift* to mankind?

And *being busy*
We mustn't let frustration harass us,
But should let it remind us instead that

JOY IS HARD BOUGHT.

It takes all our time and effort
to strive toward being what Christ can
someday make of us.

Even advertising
can remind you of Him
if you let it represent the fact
that sometimes we need to be
prodded to give—
remembering that

GOD WANTS US TO BE GIVERS.

When you bring
evergreen boughs into your home...

Do you remember that through the ages
they have been the *symbol of life*—

EVERLASTING LIFE—
brought to us by the Savior?

"Christmas is for children."
Playing Santa is special and spiritual
 when the light of excitement in a child's face
  reminds us of the vital, gentle fact of Christianity:

"OF SUCH
 IS THE KINGDOM
  OF HEAVEN."

ALL THINGS
BEAR RECORD OF HIM.

HENRY WADSWORTH LONGFELLOW
helped us discover this secret of Christmas joy
when he wrote "I Heard the Bells on Christmas Day."

Notice how his WHOLE SPIRIT LIGHTENS
as he starts to allow the symbol of the bells to
bear record to him of Christ.

I heard the bells on Christmas Day
Their old, familiar carols play,
And wild and sweet the words repeat
of peace on earth, good-will to men!

I thought how, as the day had come,
The belfries of all Christendom
Had rolled along the unbroken song
of peace on earth, good-will to men!

And in despair I bowed my head;
"there is no peace on earth," I said;
"For hate is strong, and mocks the song
of peace on earth, good-will to men!

Then pealed the bells more loud and deep:
"God is not dead; nor doth he sleep!
The Wrong shall fail, the Right prevail,
with peace on earth, good-will to men!"

Till, ringing, singing on its way,
The world revolved from night to day,
A voice, a chime, a chant sublime
of peace on earth, good-will to men!

WHAT THINK YOU OF CHRISTMAS?

Let YOUR Christmas revolve from night to day
The bells can peal more loud and deep for YOU.

God is not dead.

THERE IS CHRIST IN CHRISTMAS.

All things bear record of Him.
The joy and spirituality you can find
in the symbols of Christmas are
as limitless as the strength and range of
your testimony.

What is the range
of your testimony of Christ?

Does it include peace?

Think of eternal perspective when
you see a wreath with its
perfect round shape.

Is there love there?

Look for it in a *handmade gift*.

Our magnificent earth is the
handiwork of our Lord
and a gift to us.

Is there gratitude?

Feel it in your heart for Him
when you see it
in the eyes of another.

Follow Alma's advice: DESIRE TO BELIEVE.
The joy that the Christmas season brings into your life
will surely begin to *enlarge your soul.*

Your testimony will swell within you.
You will have *the name of Christ*
in your Christmas...

And a personal way to say with the Prophet:

"After the many testimonies which have been given of Him,
this is the testimony, last of all, which we give of Him:

THAT HE LIVES!"

Rejoice!

MERRY CHRISTMAS!